USING THE INTERNET

VALERIE BODDEN | ILLUSTRATIONS BY ELWOOD H. SMITH

CREATIVE C EDUCATION

Published by Creative Education
P.O. Box 227, Mankato, Minnesota 56002
Creative Education is an imprint of The Creative Company
www.thecreativecompany.us

Design and production by Liddy Walseth
Art direction by Rita Marshall
Printed in the United States of America

Illustrations by Elwood H. Smith © 2012

Library of Congress Cataloging-in-Publication Data

Bodden, Valerie.
Using the Internet / by Valerie Bodden.
p. cm. — (Research for writing)
Includes bibliographical references and index.
Summary: A narrative guide to conducting research on the Internet,
complete with an overview of methodologies, tips for generating
search words and evaluating sites, and helpful resources.
ISBN 978-1-60818-207-7
1. Internet research—Juvenile literature. 2. Internet searching—
Juvenile literature. 3. Computer network resources—Juvenile literature.
4. Electronic information resource literacy—Juvenile literature. I. Title.

ZA4228.B63 2012
025.042'5—dc23   2011040493

First Edition
2 4 6 8 9 7 5 3 1

TABLE OF CONTENTS

YOU CONDUCT RESEARCH EVERY DAY.
AND YOU PROBABLY DON'T EVEN REALIZE IT.

When you want to know the score of last night's football game, you check online. If you're wondering how to spell (or define) "supercilious," you get out the dictionary. And when you've forgotten the math assignment, you e-mail your friends to ask them. Although these research situations are rather informal, the skills you use for them are similar to those you need to conduct research for writing. After all, research is basically just a search—a search for sources that contain specific, **relevant**, and accurate information about your topic.

Today, many people turn to the Internet for almost all of their informational needs. Why? It's quick, it's easy, and it's chock-full of information on nearly every topic imaginable. Let's say you need to research British author J. K. Rowling, for example. You type her name into a search engine such as Google or Yahoo and—poof!—millions of results come up in less than a second. In addition to the author's official Web site, you can find newspaper and magazine articles, encyclopedia entries, pages relating to her books, and even fan discussions.

In fact, the Internet has so much information that it can be overwhelming to try to extract exactly what you need. And it can be difficult to determine whether the information you find is accurate. For those reasons, you need to learn how to conduct specific, logical Internet searches and to evaluate their results carefully. When you do, the Internet can become a powerful tool for research!

INFORMATION ON THE INTERNET

WITH SO MUCH INFORMATION AVAILABLE ON THE INTERNET, you may think it's the best place to go for every kind of research. The truth is that sometimes it is, and sometimes it isn't. If you are looking for information on current issues or breaking news, the Internet may indeed be the place to go. After all, content on a new discovery or event can be posted almost immediately—long before it makes it into print in a book or journal, and even before it appears on the printed pages of a daily newspaper. Or, if you need a specific fact or statistic, general background information on a subject, access to scientific research, or polls of public opinion, the Internet may have what you are looking for.

However, internet research has its disadvantages. Unless you know exactly what you are looking for, you may spend a lot of time clicking around on useless or irrelevant sites. This can be especially true at the beginning of the research process, before you have gained a good understanding of your topic and its key terminology. In addition, the content of the Internet changes daily. This means that a site that was there yesterday may no longer be available today, making it hard to go back and check facts you may have found earlier. Among the biggest challenges in doing Internet research is that there is no oversight, or overall supervision, on the Internet. In other words, there is no one to ensure that all sites are of high quality and contain accurate information.

The keys to conducting effective Internet research

are knowing what you are looking for, where to find it, and how to evaluate it. These skills are known as information literacy, and according to the American Library Association, a person who has mastered them has "learned how to learn." The first step in becoming information literate—and in doing any research, on the Internet or elsewhere—is to figure out what you need. This may seem obvious, but there is more to it than may at first appear. For example, if you want to research aliens, you are going to be quickly overwhelmed if you simply type that term into a search engine. You will receive millions of hits, including Web sites on movies called *Alien*, sites about alleged alien encounters, and even computer software bearing the name Alien. It could take a lifetime to sort through all the results! In order to come up with relevant sites, you need to narrow your topic. Perhaps you are interested in alien abduction stories, for example. A search for this narrowed topic will bring up a more manageable (though still considerable) list of results, with case files, videos, and more.

Once you have your topic, the next step in becoming information literate is figuring out how—and where—to research it. If you need access to a lot of information (about recycling programs in different communities, for example) or if you are looking for one specific fact (such as how many plastic bottles are thrown away in the United States every year), a search engine is probably your best online resource. You can type your search terms into a box and have the answers at your fingertips within a fraction of a second. Search engines are not the only useful research tool on the Internet, however. If you need high-quality information about a general subject area, you may decide to check out a Web directory such as the Internet Public Library (www.ipl.org) instead, since it provides links to sites that have been reviewed and categorized by human editors. And if you are looking for information and opinions from others, ranging from experts to **amateurs**, you might check out blogs or discussion groups. Don't forget that the Internet also provides access to a number of digitized resources that were once available only in print, including books, reference works, newspapers, and journal articles.

Once you have found the information you need, your job is done, right? Not so fast! An important step in the information literacy process is evaluating your sources. While evaluation is a necessary stage of all research, whether you rely on interviews, surveys, or printed books, it is especially critical when you are conducting Internet research. Why? The Internet has no "gatekeepers" to require an author to check her facts or to reject works of poor quality. In fact, many Web sites are written by people just like you, who are not experts and who may—accidentally or intentionally—post false or potentially misleading

information. So, it is up to you to verify that what a Web site says is reliable.

If your information comes from an online journal, credible newspaper or magazine, recognized reference work (such as the online version of *Encyclopaedia Britannica*), or government document, it is likely reliable, although you'll still want to look into its author's credentials and its date of publication. For many other sites, you need to be wary of accepting the information provided at face value. To begin to evaluate a site, first look for

information about its author. This may be more difficult than it sounds, since many Web sites are written anonymously. If you can find an author's name, try to figure out if she is a recognized expert in the field. Are her credentials listed? If so, check into them. If not, do a search for her name and see what you can find out about her expertise. If an e-mail address is provided, you can even write to the author to learn more about her background in the subject. Also consider the site on which the information appears. University and government Web sites tend to be reliable; **commercial** or personal sites may be less so, since they may be **biased** or one-sided. In addition, consider whether the site is current. Most sites include a "last updated" date on the bottom of the page. If the site contains information about time-sensitive issues and hasn't been updated in a year or more, it may mean that it is no longer maintained—and its information may no longer be correct.

425,425 PEOPLE DIED

As you are examining a source for reliability, also take a look at the content of the information provided. Does the author **cite** sources to back her claims? For example, she might state that 425,425 people died from heart disease in 2006. But unless she states where that fact came from (in this case, the American Heart Association), you have no way of knowing whether she took it from a reputable source—or made it up. Documenting sources is a good indication of reliability, but don't be afraid to check the sources the author cites. Make sure that they say what the author claims they say. And you can also fact-check the information against other reliable sources such as encyclopedias.

Even if a site provides reputable information, it may still be biased. Consider why the site exists. Is its purpose to sell you something or to promote a business? Is the source intended to convince you that a certain point of view is correct—maybe that animal testing is inhumane, for example? Then expect the site to give you only one side of the story. Bias is not wrong—in fact, we all have biases—but you do need to recognize a site's bias if you are going to interpret its information correctly.

In addition to reliability, also consider a source's relevance to your subject. A search engine, especially, is going to return plenty of irrelevant sites. Skip over them to find those that fill your research needs. The Internet is full of information—it's up to you to find the best of it!

THE INTERNET AND THE WORLD WIDE WEB

Although the words "Internet" and "World Wide Web" are often used interchangeably, they represent two different things. The Internet is a worldwide computer network that allows computers to communicate with one another. The World Wide Web, on the other hand, is a part of the Internet that contains documents and files, such as Web pages, that are connected to each other through hyperlinks. So, the Internet forms the foundation of the Web (as well as of e-mail and instant messaging services). The Internet originated in the late 1960s with four linked computers located at different American universities. By 1990, more than 300,000 computers were connected to the Internet. In 1991, the World Wide Web was introduced, and Internet use exploded, reaching more than 1 million computers by 1992. Today, more than 1.8 billion people around the world have access to the Internet—and the Web and other resources it supports.

FINDING YOUR WAY AROUND

UNLIKE THE LIBRARY, WITH ITS ORGANIZED CATALOGS and neatly stacked shelves, the Internet is like a big, disorganized pile of information. And you have to dig into the middle of that pile to find what you need. Internet searching sometimes takes patience, with many starts and stops and do-overs, but if you stick with it, chances are you'll manage to burrow your way to the information you need eventually.

When most people need information, they turn to search engines. These sites do just what their name implies: they search the Web for sites containing your search terms. But how? Each search engine is designed with a software program (often referred to as a spider) that "crawls" from Web page to Web page, **indexing** the terms it finds as it goes. When you perform a search, the search engine can bring up every page it has indexed that contains that specific term. Different search engines display the results of their searches according to different criteria, including the site's popularity (based on how many other sites link to the page) or where and how often your search term appears on the page. You should be aware, also, that some search engines allow companies to purchase the top positions on the results page. Often these results will appear off to the side or in a separate box.

Among the largest search engines are Google (which indexes about 20 to 30 billion pages), Yahoo (10 to 12 billion pages), and Bing (9 to 12 billion pages). Many of the pages indexed by each search engine overlap, but because each engine crawls and indexes pages slightly differently, a search on one may not yield the same results as a search on another. To maximize your results, it can be beneficial to use more than one search engine. Or, if you want to use several search engines at once, you can turn to a metasearch engine such as MetaCrawler or WebCrawler. A metasearch engine basically searches search engines, returning results from several at once. This can be an efficient way to get an overview of what is available on a topic, but bear in mind that metasearch engines return only the top results from each search

engine. As you search, you might also consider checking out some of the smaller search engines, such as Ask, AOL, or AltaVista. There are also specialized search engines available

for many fields. These search engines return results from sites related to a specific topic; iSEEK Education (education.iseek.com/iseek/home.page), for example, looks for your search terms on education-related sites.

Sometimes, the first term you enter into a search engine may not produce the information you expected. In that case, maybe you are using the wrong term. Think about **synonyms** for your subject. If you are looking for information on newspaper writing, for example, you might also try searching the term "journalism," or if you need information on murder convictions, you could also look up the word "homicide."

More often, however, you'll find that your

first search term yields too many results. In this case, you need to refine your search. Most search engines allow you to search for a phrase by placing quotation marks around two or more words. This

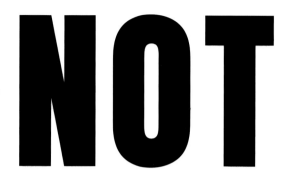

tells the search engine to return only those results in which the words appear together. If you searched for lady liberty (without quotes), for example, your results would include any pages on which the words "lady" and "liberty" both appeared. But if you searched for "lady liberty" (with quotes), your results would be limited to those pages on which the word "liberty" immediately followed the word "lady."

When you want to refine your search even further, most search engines offer the option of using **Boolean** operators. These combinations of the words "and," "or," and "not" allow you to specify exactly which words or phrases you want a page to include or exclude. So if you want to know about cuckoos—the birds, not the clocks—you might enter "cuckoo and birds not clocks." Every search engine handles Boolean searches differently. Some, such as Google, automatically insert "and" when you enter multiple words. Google also uses the minus sign (-) in place of "not" and requires capital letters to use the "or" operator. Because of these rules, it's best to check a search engine's guidelines (often labeled

"help") before conducting a Boolean search.

Most search engines also provide an "advanced search" link, which takes you to a screen that basically helps you perform the same tasks as a Boolean search. Google's advanced search, for instance, allows you to fill in a form telling the search engine to find pages that have "all these words" or to exclude pages with "any of these unwanted words." (Many search engine forms feature similar options, although some use different words to describe them.) Advanced searches may also enable you to search a specific part of the page (such as in the title), find pages updated within a certain time frame, or reach pages written at a specific reading level. In addition, some allow you to search for your terms on a specific site. So if you want an article about cuckoo birds from *National Geographic*'s Web site, for example, you could enter www.nationalgeographic.com in the field "search within site or domain" in Google's advanced search (or a similar field in another search engine).

Search engines are not the only way to find Web sites, though. Sometimes you want to access information that's a bit more organized. That's where subject directories come in. Unlike search engines, which rely on computer programs for their results, directories rely on human beings (often information experts such as editors and librarians) to compile and categorize sites. This means that they contain far fewer sites—sometimes less than one percent of the content of a major search engine—but the sites they do contain are more likely to be of high quality. In general, directories sort information into broad categories and then subdivide each category into a number of more specific topics (which are sometimes subdivided even further). Because of this, they can be useful when you are looking for general information or are trying to narrow your topic. For example, if you know that you want to research something to do with computers, you might click on the "computers" link in a subject directory to be taken to categories such as "computer literacy," "computer science," and "history of computers."

DIRECTORIES SORT INFORMATION

Many subject directories include helpful descriptions of the sites listed, and most also have search capabilities within their selected Web sites but not on the entire Web. Among the more popular subject directories are Infomine (infomine.ucr.edu), the Internet Public Library, and Open Directory (www.dmoz.org). In addition

FIGURE OUT EXACTLY WHAT YOU NEED

to these general subject directories, you can find specialized directories (or portals) for nearly any subject as well. For example, Best of History Web Sites (www.besthistorysites.net) provides links to history Web sites, broken down into categories such as "modern history," "military history," and "art history." You may be able to find a specialized directory for your topic by entering your subject term followed by the words "web directory" or "resources" in a search engine. For more general (rather than academic, or educational) information, some major search engines, such as Yahoo, also have their own subject directories. These larger directories may also contain more commercial sites. Whether you use a search engine or a directory, once you get to a site, you may find that it provides helpful links to many other relevant sites. Clicking from one to another (an action known as browsing, or surfing) may yield results. So don't wander the Web aimlessly. Figure out exactly what you need and then conduct a search that will find it!

PRACTICE MAKES PERFECT

Although you may search the Internet regularly (maybe even daily), searching for research purposes takes practice. You need to come up with terms that will give you appropriate results—and leave out as many irrelevant ones as possible. First, think of a general subject, such as Australia or food or space. Go to a search engine such as Google and type in your term. How many results do you get? Way too many! To help narrow your topic, visit a Web directory, such as the Internet Public Library. Click on the subject headings until you find a specific topic that looks interesting—maybe snorkeling Australia's Great Barrier Reef, for example. Now go back to the search engine and use Boolean operators or the advanced search option to refine your search. If you still have too many results, narrow your topic again and refine your search even further. Do the results appear to be relevant and reliable now?

REACHING
THE RESOURCES

THE WORLD WIDE WEB IS MADE UP OF MORE than just the Web sites of individuals, institutions, and organizations. It is also filled with works that were once available only in print. In addition, the Web has numerous audiovisual resources, as well as gathering spaces where you can "talk" to—and learn from—other people who are interested in a specific field.

While you once may have had to travel to the library to use reference books such as dictionaries and encyclopedias, today many are just a click away. Sites such as Onelook.com provide access to several free online dictionaries. Or, you can visit the sites of specific dictionaries individually. A number of print encyclopedias also offer online versions. Some, such as *Encyclopaedia Britannica*, charge a subscription fee for full access (although you can see parts of articles for free), while others are accessible only through a library's subscription (check a local library's Web site to see if it offers access to any online reference works). Online encyclopedias often offer features not available in the print versions, such as Web links, audiovisual materials, and frequent updates. If you are looking for a brief entry on a subject, you might visit Encyclopedia.com, which offers the contents of the *Columbia Encyclopedia* and other reference works for free. If you need an almanac, atlas, or other handbook, you can check out the CIA World Factbook (for maps and statistical information on the countries of the world), Infoplease.com (providing almanacs, atlases, and encyclopedias), or Census.gov (statistical information about the U.S. population).

Today, an increasing number of books are also available online. Sites such as Project Gutenberg (www.gutenberg.org) and Bartleby.com offer thousands of free e-books, most of them published before 1920 and therefore in the public domain (meaning they are no longer under **copyright** protection). Many libraries also offer access to newer e-books through either their own Web sites or **databases** such as NetLibrary.

When you need information on breaking news topics or current events, one of your best sources may be the Web site of a newspaper or magazine. In some cases, you can obtain information on a newspaper's Web site even before the print version of the paper has gone to press. And the Internet provides access to everything from small hometown newspapers to major national and international news sources. Many newspapers and magazines offer at least part of their content free online, although you may have to purchase a subscription for full access. In addition, a number of sites have placed their **archives** online. *The New York Times*'s site, for example, allows you to search its archives for articles dating back to 1851, although there is a fee to access the full text of many articles. Most libraries also offer online databases containing summaries or even the full texts of articles from major

LIBRARY DATABASES

newspapers and magazines from around the country and the world.

Library databases usually include articles from journals as well. These academic resources tend to offer the latest scholarship on a subject, and since their articles are reviewed by experts in the field, they are among the most authoritative and up-to-date sources in many subject areas. Outside library databases, some journals (even many in languages other than

English) can be accessed on sites such as the Directory of Open Access Journals (www.doaj.org) or Jurn.org.

Because journal articles are stored within databases, you may not find

them by using a basic search engine. That's because databases are part of what is called the "invisible" Web, or the "deep" Web. These are sites that are invisible to search engine spiders, either because they are protected by passwords or because their content is in a format that spiders cannot read, such as an entry in a database. The good news is that you can still get to sites on the invisible Web. Try typing your keywords followed by the word "database" in a search engine. For example, if you are looking for information on natural disasters, you might enter "natural disaster database" into a search engine. Or you can try using a search engine designed specifically for the invisible Web, such as CompletePlanet, which provides access to more than 70,000 databases. You may not be able to access the content of all the databases you find, since some will be available only by subscription or with a password, but the articles you are able to access are likely to contain high-quality, topic-specific information.

If, instead of articles relating to a topic, you are looking for **primary sources**, such as copies of original historical documents or **artifacts**, the

Internet may also have what you need. Many museums, archives, and historical institutions have placed digital copies of their primary sources online. The Library of Congress's American Memory site (memory.loc.gov), for example, provides access to documents and photographs relating to American history. You can find everything from a copy of Thomas Jefferson's original draft of the Declaration of Independence to images of early baseball cards. And Yale Law School's Avalon Project (avalon.law.yale.edu) provides primary documents related to history, law, and **diplomacy** from ancient through modern times. For topics concerning recent laws or public policy, other sites, such as the U.S. Government Printing Office's catalog of government publications (catalog.gpo.gov), provide access to relevant records.

As you conduct your Internet search, don't overlook non-print resources such as video footage or audio recordings. Many radio and television news stations make archived programs available online, for example. Such programs can give you access to interviews with public figures or a firsthand view of world-changing events. Most search engines provide a way to search for images or videos alone (check above or alongside the search bar for such options).

For some topics, you might also seek eyewitness information from a blog. Short for "Weblog," a blog is basically an online journal kept by an individual. Although many blogs contain information that means little to anyone but the author, others can be useful for learning what life is like in a remote or dangerous part of the world or for getting firsthand information from important leaders. You can find blogs by relief workers providing aid in the African country of Sudan, for example, or by journalists working in the

Middle Eastern country of Iraq. In addition, members of the White House staff keep several blogs, with updates on what's going on in the federal government. A number of blogs are also devoted to a specific topic, such as science or journalism, and can help keep you informed of the latest developments in that field. Several search engines, such as Google Blogs (blogsearch.google.com) and Technorati (technorati.com), allow you to search blogs and their posts. Or just type your subject terms followed by the word "blog" in a general search engine. As you read blogs, however, remember that they often contain the opinions of their authors—so beware of potential bias, and be sure to verify the information you find.

Other Internet resources can also provide you with access to public opinions. Message boards, forums, and discussion groups allow people to post messages to which other people can respond. You can find groups on almost any topic, from the treatment of brain tumors to travel tips. It can be difficult to verify the identity of those who have posted to a discussion group, since most rely on **screen names**, so be sure to double-check any information you find. For many groups, you need to become a member before you can post your own comments or questions. To find a group, you can visit Yahoo Groups (groups.yahoo.com) or another group search engine, or type the words "discussion group" or "forum" after your search term in a general search engine. As you get to know the Web's many resources, you may be surprised to discover all the places in which you can find information about your topic!

A BIG, INVISIBLE WORLD

When you search a computer database, the results are generated in "real time." That is why general search engines cannot bring up articles and other content buried within databases. Search engines may be able to get you to the first pages of such sites, but they cannot take you directly to the content because they cannot enter keywords into the site's search box. Thus, this information is "invisible" to the search engine. Since the invisible Web is not indexed (which is what makes it invisible in the first place), no one knows exactly how big it is. But computer experts believe that it may be anywhere from 200 to 500 or more times larger than the visible Web. So if the visible, or indexed, Web consists of 20 billion Web pages, the invisible Web could contain 4 to 10 trillion pages—or more!

BE SITE SAVVY

MOST WEB SITES OFFER FREE CONTENT, obviously a plus when you're looking for information. After all, if you had to pay for every site you went to, you probably wouldn't visit many sites. When you're looking for high-quality information, though, sometimes it pays to pay. Online journals and encyclopedias often charge a fee, for example, but the information they provide tends to be authoritative and reliable. The same goes for many online newspapers and magazines. Other fee-based sites may provide **genealogy** records, company profiles, or other information. These sites vary in quality, so it's wise to read reviews before handing over money to see their contents.

In contrast to fee-based sites, open-content sites allow anyone to not only access their content but also to change it. Probably the best-known and most-used open-content Web site is Wikipedia, a free online encyclopedia begun in 2001 and now containing more than 3.6 million articles in English (along with millions more in other languages), all written and edited by Wikipedia users. Unlike print encyclopedias, Wikipedia offers continuous updates to the site as users add and change information based on current events. For example, an article about the 2007 Wimbledon Championships was updated daily during the 13-day tennis tournament— and continued to be updated into 2011. In addition, Wikipedia covers a number of subjects dealing

37

with popular culture—including celebrities, movies, and television shows—that are not treated in traditional encyclopedias.

The fact that Wikipedia articles can be written and edited by anyone has proven to be both an advantage and a disadvantage. Since so many people read and contribute to each article, the quality of an article may increase over time, as users correct errors and add new information. In fact, Wikipedia users have designated more than 3,000 of the site's highest-quality articles as "featured articles." (Look for a small star in the top right-hand corner of these

ARTICLES CAN BE WRITTEN BY ANYONE

articles.) At the same time, however, the openness of Wikipedia means that many articles are written by amateurs with no expertise in a given subject area. Some article writers conduct little or no research—and others even include deliberately misleading or biased information.

Even when users do conduct research, they may not document their sources, or the sources they cite may not be reliable.

Because of these disadvantages, you should never use Wikipedia as your sole source for information. (Then again, you should never use any source—whether it is a book, an article, or an interview—as your sole source.) This does not mean, however, that you need to avoid Wikipedia altogether. The site can be useful for finding information on general topics that don't require an expert's knowledge, searching out an odd fact, or getting an overview of your topic before you look for other resources. If an article cites its sources, it can also be a great way to find more information on the topic.

Even so, you need to be extra vigilant about evaluating the reliability of articles you find on Wikipedia. Most are written by anonymous contributors, so you probably won't be able to check the author's credentials. This means that you'll need to pay special attention to the content of the article. Among the first things to note is whether it cites sources. If not, be wary. If so, check into those sources. Are they reliable? Do they say what the article claims they say? Check the information in the article against outside

sources as well. Does it stand up? Is it biased? Checking the page's history (by clicking on the "view history" link at the top right-hand corner of the page) can also be useful at this point. This will take you to a page showing the history of the article's development, including conversations among users about the site's content. This can alert you to any aspects of the article that users may dispute or see as biased.

If you visit Wikipedia, you will notice that its URL (short for uniform resource locator), or address, ends in .org. This means that it is sponsored by an organization (the **nonprofit** Wikimedia Foundation). Every Web site has a URL—and that URL can tell you a lot about the site. The first part of the URL (often "http://") simply tells the web browser how to communicate with the **server** on which the Web site is stored. The next portion (often "www") refers to that server. This is followed by the domain name, or the site's name, and then the top-level domain (TLD), such as .com or .gov, which tells you what kind of site you are visiting. Often, the TLD is the key to revealing the purpose of the site. You are probably already familiar with hundreds of sites that end in .com, from Amazon.com to Facebook.com. In general, .com denotes a commercial or business site, but any site can use a .com TLD. Although the purpose of a .com site may be to sell you something or to make money, that does not necessarily mean the site is useless for research. In fact, some .com sites are strictly factual. *Encyclopaedia Britannica*'s URL ends in .com, for example, since it exists to provide a service for a fee. However, you often need to carefully evaluate the information you find on a .com site. If you are looking for statistics about video games and fitness, for example, the information you find on a video game manufacturer's Web site might differ from what is reported in a scientific study. Even if a .com site doesn't appear to be trying to sell you something directly, it may rely on ads placed throughout the site to generate money from advertisers.

In contrast, sites ending in .edu (educational institutions) or .gov (government entities) are typically ad-free. Both .edu and .gov sites tend to be reliable sources of information. URLs ending with .org are generally sponsored by nonprofit organizations. Their purpose may be to provide information for professionals in a field. The American Chemical Society, for

example, provides information related to the science of chemistry. Other .org sites **advocate** for a specific cause or comment upon the activities of an organization. Be sure to examine the purpose of a .org site before using its information. After all, if an organization exists to advocate gun control, then its site is going to present information on the benefits of gun control.

No matter what type of Web site you rely on for your information, be sure to use that information fairly. You might be tempted to think that because you found something on an anonymous Web site, you are free to use it as your own, but you are not. Information—including words, images, movies, and more—published on the Internet enjoys the same copyright privileges as information published in print or distributed on film. So as you research, make careful note of each resource's author, title, sponsoring organization, date last updated, and URL. Some of this information may be difficult (or impossible) to find for certain sites, but do your best to track down as much as you can. And when you incorporate your research into your writing, be sure to cite where it came from. If you use someone else's direct words—from a Web site or anywhere else—put them in quotation marks.

The Internet is big—so big that it's easy to get lost. But if you know where to look, you can find information on just about any subject imaginable. Some of that information will be accurate, some will not. Some will be relevant, some will not. But if you take the time to make a careful search, browse the right resources, and evaluate everything you find, you are likely to end up with information you can use. And that's the whole idea. So start clicking!

ACTIVE RESEARCH

WIKIVALUATION

With more than 3.6 million articles, Wikipedia might seem like the perfect source for all your research needs. But before you turn to it, you need to practice evaluating the content of the site's articles. Begin by visiting one of the site's featured articles (click the "featured content" link on the left-hand side of the homepage, en.wikipedia.org). Take note of the article's citations. How many are there? Are they from reputable sources? Also spot-check some of the article's facts against another source, such as a print encyclopedia. Now search for another topic—perhaps a current event or celebrity. Does this article provide reputable citations? Spot-check the facts in this article, too. (If the topic is too recent to be covered in an encyclopedia, you may want to rely on national newspapers, international news services, or the like.) Finally, compare your evaluations of the two articles. Would one be a more reliable source for a research project?

GLOSSARY

advocate—to support or promote an idea, cause, or person

amateurs—people who are not experts or professionals in a given area and who work for pleasure rather than payment

archives—collections of documents or items of historical importance, or the buildings (or online locations) where such documents or items are stored

artifacts—objects made by humans (as opposed to naturally occurring objects)

biased—having a preference for or dislike of a certain person or idea that prevents one from making impartial judgments of that person or idea

Boolean—a system of logic that combines the words "and," "or," and "not" to establish relationships between terms and ideas

cite—to quote someone else's work as evidence for an idea or argument

commercial—existing for the purpose of making money

copyright—the legal right of an author or artist to exclusively publish or reproduce his or her works

databases—organized collections of data, or information, stored on a computer

diplomacy—relationships between different nations and their leaders

genealogy—the study of family history

hyperlinks—words, images, or other items on a Web page that can be clicked on to reach other items on the same or a different Web page

indexing—in the context of the Internet, making a catalog or list of specific items, such as terms on a Web page, that can later be used to locate that Web page

network—a system of linked computers that can communicate with one another

nonprofit—existing to provide a service without making a profit (more money than is spent)

primary sources—sources that provide firsthand information, without interpretation or analysis by a secondary author

relevant—related or connected to the idea or topic being discussed

screen names—made-up names used for communicating online

server—a computer that provides services and stores files that can be accessed by other computers in a network

synonyms—words that have the same (or nearly the same) meaning

WEB SITES

American Memory from the Library of Congress

http://memory.loc.gov/ammem/index.html

Select a topic to perform general searches or practice using specific search terms to find materials.

How Stuff Works: How Internet Search Engines Work

http://computer.howstuffworks.com/internet/basics/search-engine.htm

Get an in-depth description of how search engines work.

Internet Public Library

www.ipl.org

Explore the collections and resources housed in the Internet Public Library.

TIME for Kids

http://www.timeforkids.com/TFK/kids/hh/rr

Browse useful research sites for kids—compiled by kids—for homework help.

SELECTED BIBLIOGRAPHY

Ballenger, Bruce. *The Curious Researcher: A Guide to Writing Research Papers*. New York: Pearson Longman, 2004.

Booth, Wayne C., Gregory G. Colomb, and Joseph M. Williams. *The Craft of Research*. Chicago: University of Chicago Press, 2008.

Boswell, Wendy. *The About.com Guide to Online Research*. Avon, Mass.: Adams Media, 2007.

Hock, Randolph. *The Extreme Searcher's Internet Handbook*. Medford, N.J.: CyberAge Books, 2007.

MLA Handbook for Writers of Research Papers. New York: The Modern Language Association of America, 2009.

Radford, Marie L., Susan B. Barnes, and Linda R. Barr. *Web Research: Selecting, Evaluating, and Citing*. Boston: Allyn & Bacon, 2006.

Rodrigues, Dawn, and Raymond J. Rodrigues. *The Research Paper: A Guide to Library and Internet Research*. Upper Saddle River, N.J.: Prentice Hall, 2003.

Toronto Public Library. *The Research Virtuoso: Brilliant Methods for Normal Brains*. Toronto: Annick Press, 2006.

INDEX